ME AND MY FAMILY TREE

by Joan Sweeney   illustrated by Annette Cable

Dragonfly Books® Crown Publishers, Inc. • New York

Also by Joan Sweeney and Annette Cable

ME ON THE MAP

ME AND MY PLACE IN SPACE

ME AND MY AMAZING BODY

ME COUNTING TIME: FROM SECONDS TO CENTURIES

For Patty, a very special branch of our family tree—J. S.

In memory of Alan—A.C.

DRAGONFLY BOOKS® PUBLISHED BY CROWN PUBLISHERS, INC.

Text copyright © 1999 by Joan Sweeney
Illustrations copyright © 1999 by Annette Cable

Published by Crown Publishers, Inc., a Random House company,
201 East 50th Street, New York, NY 10022

www.randomhouse.com/kids

Library of Congress Cataloging-in-Publication Data
Sweeney, Joan, 1930–
Me and my family tree / by Joan Sweeney ; illustrated by Annette Cable.
p.   cm.
Summary: Using a family tree, a child explains how her brother, parents, grandparents,
aunts, uncles, and cousins are related to her.
1. Genealogy—Juvenile literature. 2. Family—Juvenile literature.
[1. Genealogy.] I. Cable, Annette, ill. II. Title.
CS15.5.S94   1999
929'.1—dc21   97-44201

ISBN   0-517-70966-X (trade)
0-517-70967-8 (lib. bdg.)
0-517-88597-2 (pbk.)

First Dragonfly Books® edition: April 2000

Printed in Singapore

10 9 8 7 6 5 4 3

This is me and my family.

I have a brother, a mommy and a daddy, grandparents,
aunts and uncles, and cousins too.
How are they all related to me?
I'll show you on my family tree.

First I start with me.

Then comes my big brother, Alan.

We're both part of my family tree.

These are my parents—
my mommy and daddy.

They're part of my family tree.

This is my mommy's
mommy—my grandma.

This is my mommy's
daddy—my grandpa.

This is my daddy's
mommy—my nana.

This is my daddy's
daddy—my poppa.

They're all part of my family tree.

Mommy has a sister—my Aunt Sally. She's married to my
Uncle Lee. They have a daughter—my cousin Alice.

They're all part of my family tree.

Daddy has a brother—my Uncle Jim. He's married to my Aunt Margie. They have two sons—my cousin Jeff and my cousin David. Daddy also has a sister—that's my Aunt Pat.

They're *all* part of my family tree.
Now—can you guess how I came to be?

Grandma and Grandpa had Mommy and her sister.

the championship 1973

Ride 'em Cowboy

to Mark

Mark, 1972

Nana and Poppa had Daddy and his brother and sister.

Baby David, Jan. 14, 1991

My aunts and uncles
had my cousins.

Alice

Sallie, Lee and Alice, 1994

Mommy and Daddy
had my brother.

And then . . . Mommy and Daddy had *me!*

One day I may have children, and
they'll be part of my family tree.

Think of it! Everyone in the world has a family tree.

Just like you and me.

My Family

Grandma & Grandpa

Grandma & Grandpa

aunts & uncles

aunts & uncles

Mommy

Daddy

cousins

cousins

brothers

me

sisters